Contents

Invaders and settlers

People who make their home in a new land are called 'settlers'.

'Invaders' are people who attack someone else's land and try to take it over.

Sometimes people start as invaders and end up as settlers. They attack someone else's land and then decide to live on it.

Two thousand years ago the people who lived in Britain were called 'Celts' or 'Britons'. They were farmers and fighters. They lived lived in large groups, or tribes. Each tribe had its own ruler.

Over the next thousand years three lots of invaders and settlers arrived in Britain.

First came the Romans. Then the Anglo-Saxons. Then the Vikings.

We know about them from the things they left behind.

two thousand years ago   one thousand years ago   today

300   200   100   **BC** **AD**   100   200   300   400   500   600   700   800   900   1000   1500

AD 43
Romans

AD 250
Anglo-Saxons

AD 874
Vikings

This is Hadrian's Wall. The Romans who lived in Britain built it nearly two thousand years ago. It is four metres high, and wide enough to walk on. It runs for one hundred and thirty kilometres across the north of England.

2

The Anglo-Saxons built the tower of this church. We know they built in this style. The rest of the church was re-built later.

A Viking leather-worker made these shoes.

Archaeologists found them buried in York.

Most Romans could read and write. So could some Anglo-Saxons and Vikings. They wrote on stone and on **parchment scrolls**.

So we can also find out about them from what they wrote and from the stories and records of what they did.

Archaeologist

Someone who finds out about the past from clues buried under the ground.

Parchment scroll

Parchment is made from sheep skins. A roll of parchment or paper is called a scroll.

The Roman Empire

The Romans came from the city of Rome in Italy. They were very good at fighting as well as building. Just over two thousand years ago their armies took over all the other towns in Italy. Then they invaded the lands of people living outside Italy.

The lands they ruled were called the 'Roman **Empire**'. You can see it marked on this map.

The Roman Empire in AD 117

Empire

A group of countries ruled by one country.

How the Romans came to Britain

A Roman general called Julius Caesar was fighting in France. He crossed the sea to Britain with an army.

He found that Britain was a rich country with supplies of lead, tin and silver.

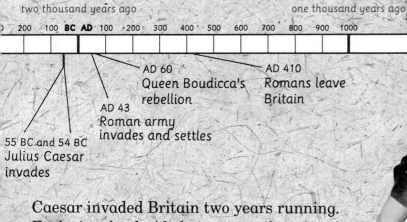

two thousand years ago   one thousand years ago   today

200 100 **BC AD** 100 200 300 400 500 600 700 800 900 1000   1500

AD 60
Queen Boudicca's rebellion

AD 410
Romans leave Britain

AD 43
Roman army invades and settles

55 BC and 54 BC
Julius Caesar invades

Caesar invaded Britain two years running. Each time he decided not to stay because the Britons were fierce fighters.

A hundred years later, the **Emperor** Claudius wanted to make the Roman Empire bigger. He ordered his army to invade Britain. This time the Romans took Britain over. They ruled it for three hundred and fifty years and many Roman soldiers settled there.

The story that follows is about real people. It tells how some of the Britons tried to get rid of the Romans. We know about it because Roman writers wrote down what happened. The Britons could not write, so we do not have their side of the story.

Emperor

Chief ruler of an empire.

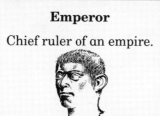

5   Model of a Roman soldier

One tribe, called the Iceni, did not fight the Romans when they invaded Britain. As a reward the Romans allowed their king to go on ruling, and they left the tribe in peace.

Twenty years later, the king died. So the Roman Emperor sent an officer called Catus to take over all his land and wealth.

The king's wife, Boudicca, and her two daughters were at the royal palace when Catus arrived.

Boudicca was a tall woman. Her bright red hair hung down to her knees. She wore a dress of many colours, and over it a thick cloak held together by a brooch.

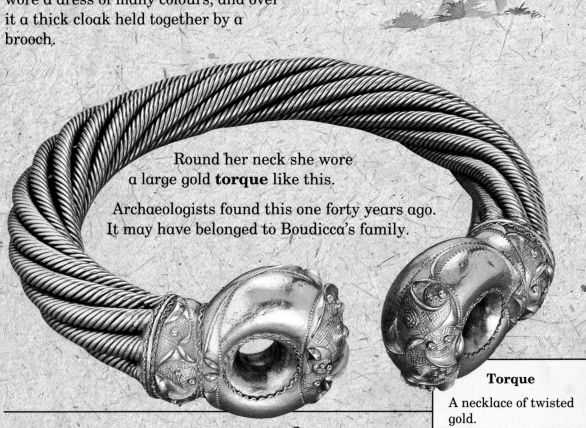

Round her neck she wore a large gold **torque** like this.

Archaeologists found this one forty years ago. It may have belonged to Boudicca's family.

Torque

A necklace of twisted gold.

Catus and his men started to search the palace for the royal family's gold and silver.

Boudicca was angry. She expected to be treated like a queen. She said they had no right to do this. When she tried to stop them, Catus ordered his men to whip her.

When the Iceni heard about this they started to attack the Romans. Other tribes joined them and together they marched to the Roman city of Colchester.

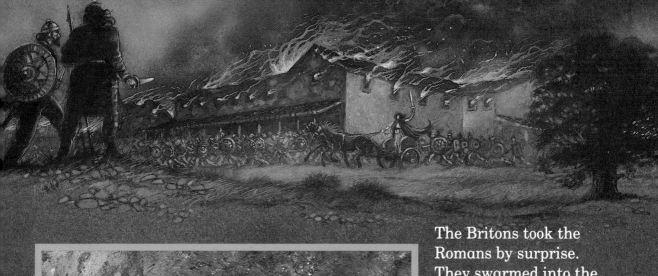

The Britons took the Romans by surprise. They swarmed into the city and set it on fire. Everything was badly burnt, even these dates.

Archaeologists found them thirty years ago. Dates do not grow in Britain, so the Romans probably had them sent from Palestine, where modern Israel and Jordan are today.

Next the Britons marched on London. They could not wait to get their revenge on the Romans. They cut their throats. They hung them. They burned their houses.

Then Boudicca led them out of London towards the Roman army. The Britons were so sure they would win, they brought their families to watch the battle.

They drove their carts into a great half-circle round the battlefield, with the women and children standing in them to get a good view.

Boudicca rode round her army in a chariot. It probably looked like this model.

"We British are used to women commanders in war," she said. "But I am not fighting for my **kingdom** and wealth. I am fighting to be free."

Kingdom

Land ruled by a king or queen.

There were ten Britons to every one Roman. But the Roman general knew that his soldiers were well trained and well armed. They each had two throwing spears, called javelins, a shield, and a sword.

Suddenly trumpets sounded, and thousands of Britons rushed at them. When they were fifty metres away, all the Romans moved at once like a machine. Six thousand javelins flew through the air. Then six thousand more. The first line of Britons fell.

Then the Romans moved close together, pulled out their swords, and, with a great shout, charged.

After many hours, the Romans won. Some Britons escaped but the Romans killed everyone they caught, even the families who were watching.

Boudicca poisoned herself. The Romans were back in charge.

The battle between the Romans and the Britons probably looked like this.

The carving is by a Roman artist.

The Anglo-Saxons arrived in Britain in boats like this.

They came across the North Sea from Germany.

At first they came as **raiders**. They stole from the Romans and Britons and then sailed home again.

The Romans built special forts on the sea-shore to try to keep them out. Then the Roman Emperor ordered his army to leave Britain. He needed it to defend Rome, which was being attacked by other tribes.

This made it easy for the Anglo-Saxons to land.

They were farmers as well as sailors. But they found it difficult to grow enough food because their land in Germany was covered in woods and marshes.

So they decided to settle in Britain where the land was better.

Anglo-Saxon Britain around AD 600

Norway

Swed

Scotland

NORTH SEA

Denmark

Ireland

Wales   England

Germany

Netherlands

Belgium

France

They sailed up rivers and settled on the land beside them. As more and more Anglo-Saxons arrived they started to spread out across Britain.

Raiders

People who make a sudden attack on a place, stealing and causing damage.

The Britons fought many battles to try to stop them. But in the end the Anglo-Saxons managed to drive them off all the land except in Wales, Devon and Cornwall.

The Anglo-Saxons called their part of Britain 'England' and started to call themselves the 'English'. The English language spoken today comes from their language.

But England was not one country like it is now. To begin with there were seven different Anglo-Saxon kingdoms. Each one had its own king or queen.

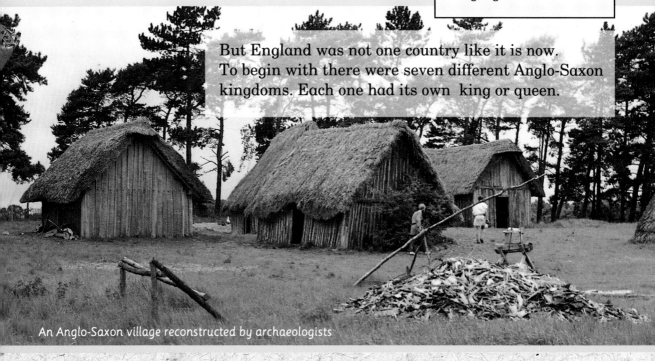

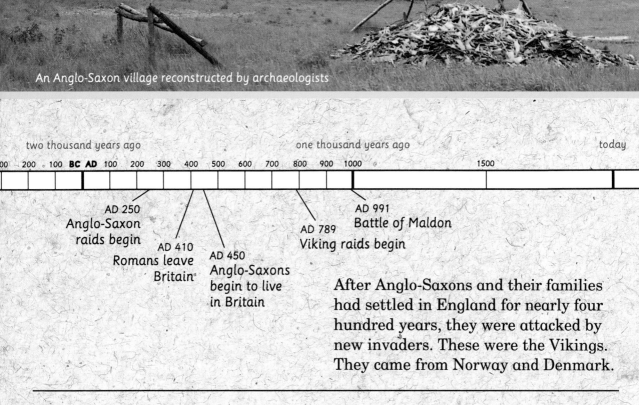

An Anglo-Saxon village reconstructed by archaeologists

two thousand years ago   one thousand years ago   today

00 200 100 **BC AD** 100 200 300 400 500 600 700 800 900 1000 1500

AD 250
Anglo-Saxon
raids begin

AD 410
Romans leave
Britain

AD 450
Anglo-Saxons
begin to live
in Britain

AD 789
Viking raids begin

AD 991
Battle of Maldon

After Anglo-Saxons and their families had settled in England for nearly four hundred years, they were attacked by new invaders. These were the Vikings. They came from Norway and Denmark.

The Battle of Maldon

The Anglo-Saxons fought against the Vikings at the Battle of Maldon. We know about it because an Anglo-Saxon poet wrote down what happened.

At the time when Ethelred was king of the English, some Viking raiders sailed up the River Blackwater in Essex. They landed on an island and made a camp.

As soon as the English people living there saw this, they sent a message to tell the king's chief man in the area. His name was Byrhtnoth.

Byrhtnoth's job was to make sure that all the men in Essex were ready to fight for the king. He was their leader in war. He was old now, but he was a good soldier who had seen many battles.

He had promised to be loyal to the king in a special **ceremony**. Here is an Anglo-Saxon picture of what happened.

Ceremony

A special occasion when important things take place.

As soon as Byrhtnoth heard the news about the Vikings, he sent messengers to every village to call his men together.

Some were young **thanes**. They rode to battle on horses. Each carried a spear, a shield and a sword. One of them had trained a hawk to hunt for him. It perched on his wrist as he rode along.

Other men were farmers. They usually worked in the fields like this.

Thane

A rich person who owned a lot of land.

Now they all marched off to meet Byrhtnoth carrying their spears, shields and bows and arrows. They could not all afford a sword as they were very expensive.

All these men had sworn to follow Byrhtnoth and never let him down.

When Byrhtnoth's army reached the river, he told each soldier to get off his horse and drive it away. Then the young men realised that this was to be a fight to the death. Byrhtnoth would not allow them to retreat.

The one with the hawk let it fly up to perch in a tree and wait for him there.

Byrhtnoth showed his men where to stand to hold off the enemy. He showed them how to hold their shields firm and how to stand close together and not move.

Then a Viking messenger came to the edge of the island and called over the water. "If you give us gold," he shouted, "we will go away without fighting."

The Vikings were always on the look out for gold. This Viking treasure was found in Norway.

Some of it came from Britain, some from places in France and Germany, and some from as far away as Constantinople, now called Istanbul, in Turkey.

Byrhtnoth was angry. "Listen," he shouted back. "We will pay you alright. We will pay you with the points of our spears and the edges of our trusty swords. Tell your people that we stand here ready to guard this country. We will defend our people and their land."

Then he told his men to move up to the water's edge and make a wall with their shields.

A single pathway joined the island to the river bank where they stood. He told three men to guard it.

The Vikings knew they could never get past, so they shouted to Byrhtnoth to let them wade over.

If he said 'no', they would have to give up and sail away. Instead, he called out, "We will let you cross. Come quickly to meet us in battle."

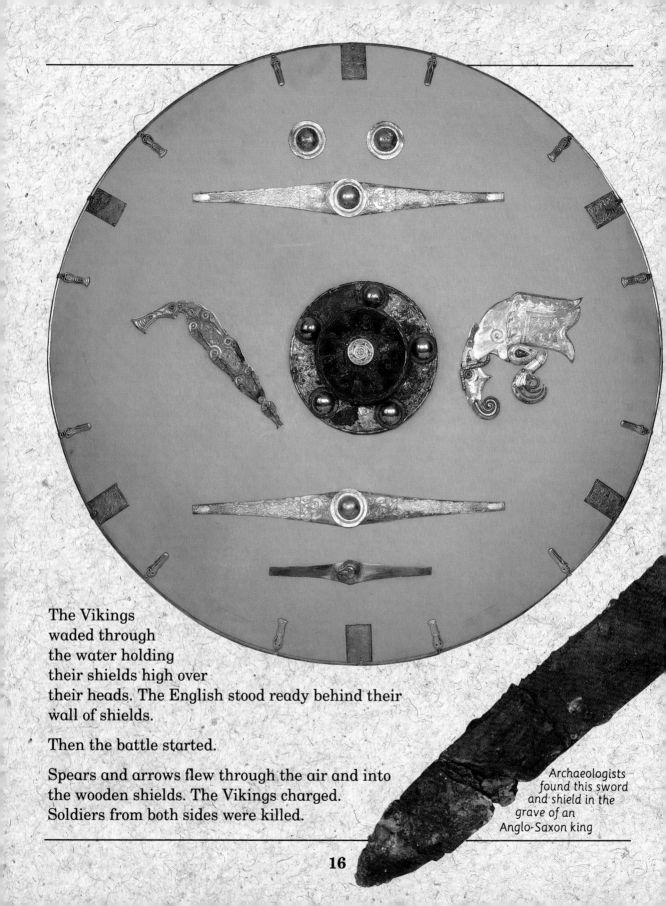

The Vikings
waded through
the water holding
their shields high over
their heads. The English stood ready behind their
wall of shields.

Then the battle started.

Spears and arrows flew through the air and into
the wooden shields. The Vikings charged.
Soldiers from both sides were killed.

Archaeologists
found this sword
and shield in the
grave of an
Anglo-Saxon king

Twice Byrhtnoth was hit by spears. Then a well armed Viking came up. He wanted the general's fine gold rings and his precious sword with its golden handle. It was the most valuable thing he owned.

Byrhtnoth drew the sword and killed the Viking. But then another of them leapt up and smashed the old man's arm. His sword fell to the ground.

As he fell the white haired general still urged his men on. Then he looked up and prayed to God that he should enter Heaven peacefully.

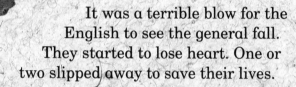

It was a terrible blow for the English to see the general fall. They started to lose heart. One or two slipped away to save their lives.

Then one of the young thanes gave them new strength. "Don't forget how we swore to obey our leader," he called out.

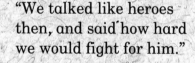

"We talked like heroes then, and said how hard we would fight for him."

They fought on grimly. But one by one they fell, worn out by their wounds.

They fought to the last man. The Vikings took all the valuable weapons and jewels from the dead bodies of the English. Then they buried their own dead and sailed away.

This carving comes from the front of a Viking ship. It looks very fierce. That is how people always remember the Vikings. They were good sailors and fierce fighters.

But there was another side to the Vikings. The carving is a clue to it. They were good at making things and they were good artists.

The Vikings came from Norway, Sweden and Denmark where they lived by the sea on little farms. But there was not enough good land for all of them to make a living.

So some of them used their long, fast boats to make **raids** on other lands. Most of all they wanted gold and jewels. They also stole food and drink and animals. Then they sailed home.

But they got tired of sailing home every time. They wanted to settle in the lands they raided.

Raid

A sudden attack on a place, when people steal and cause damage.

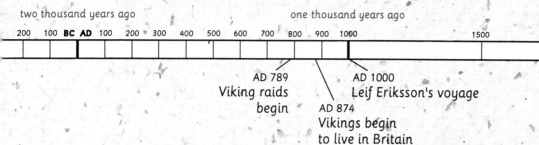

AD 789
Viking raids
begin

AD 874
Vikings begin
to live in Britain

AD 1000
Leif Eriksson's voyage

The Vikings raided England for many years before they decided to invade. Then a large army arrived from Denmark.

It took over most of the Anglo-Saxon kingdoms. Only Alfred who was king of Wessex, a big kingdom in the south, managed to hold out against them.

In the end, the Vikings agreed not to attack Wessex. They settled down to live among the Anglo-Saxons in the north and east of England.

Other Vikings settled in France and Russia. Some sailed further than anyone had been before and settled in Iceland and Greenland.

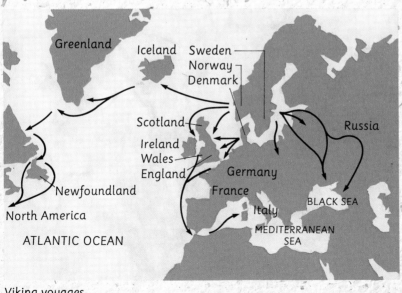

Viking voyages

The Vikings were the first people from Europe to reach America. We know about this because the Vikings liked to tell the stories of their voyages. They called them 'sagas' and long afterwards someone wrote them down.

How the Vikings sailed to America

This is Greenland. It is green in the summer. In the winter it is white with ice and snow.

A thousand years ago, a Viking called Leif Eriksson lived here. His stone farm house has fallen down now, but you can see where it used to stand on the flat ground beside the water.

One day a sailor called Bjarni arrived in Greenland. He told Leif how he had just sailed hundreds of miles from Iceland. He said a storm had blown him off course on the way and he had seen another country with low hills covered by trees.

Leif decided to go and explore this new land. He bought Bjarni's ship and asked thirty-five other men to go with him.

First they had to get the ship ready.

They loaded it with food and drink. They took meat, bread and cheese, and fresh water in wooden barrels.

When all was ready they put to sea. At night they slept in their clothes, rolled up in animal skins and furs. But they got soaking wet because there was nowhere to hide from the spray of the sea.

One day they sighted land. Far inland they could see high, snowy mountains. Between the sea and the mountains there was nothing but rock.

Leif said, "I shall give this land a name. We will call it 'Helluland', the land of rocks."

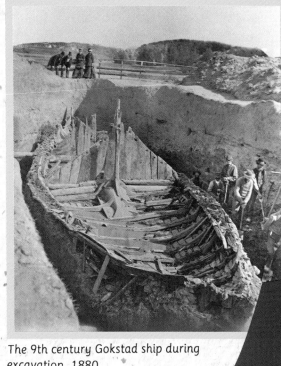

The 9th century Gokstad ship during excavation, 1880

The ship probably looked like this one which is now in a museum in Norway.

Archaeologists found it buried in mud a hundred years ago.

You can see holes along the side for oars and a place in the middle for a mast.

Then they sailed away and found another land. This one was flat and covered with trees. Leif said, "We will call this 'Markland', the land of forests."

They sailed on. This time a gale blew them along for two days. When it stopped, they saw an island. They went ashore and found a lake.

They decided to make a camp. They unpacked the ship and set up their tents.

They decided to stay for the winter, so they built a big house.

When they explored the island they found grapes growing there. You can make wine from grapes. So Leif called the island 'Vinland', the land of wine.

When spring came, they packed up and sailed for home.

The Vikings carried things like these on board the ship.

Archaeologists reconstructed these Viking huts and boat houses in Newfoundland using the remains they found as clues.

They are made of stone and turf. Turf is earth with the grass and its roots still in it.

This is part of the island of Newfoundland, next to the coast of North America.

Forty years ago archaeologists found the remains of some Vikings' huts and boat houses here. They also found this metal dress pin with a ring in the top.

The Vikings used pins like this. So this may be where Leif and his men built their camp.

Perhaps this pin belonged to one of them.

actual size

The last invader

One more invader came to Britain after the Vikings. His name was William, Duke of Normandy.

Normandy means 'land of the northmen'. It is the part of France where the Vikings settled and it was named after them. Duke William could trace his family back to the Vikings. He invaded England in 1066, just over nine hundred years ago. England had become one country by then.

King Harold

William said that Edward, the Anglo-Saxon king, had promised that he should be the next king. But when Edward died the English chose an **earl** called Harold as king instead.

So William set sail with a big army. Here are some of his ships.

William defeated Harold at the battle of Hastings and was crowned king.

Many new settlers have come to Britain since those days. But so far there have been no more invaders.

Earl

The title of an English nobleman.